True Survival

ADA BLACKJACK

CASTAWAY

Virginia Loh-Hagan

⊙ 45th Parallel Press

Published in the United States of America by Cherry Lake Publishing
Ann Arbor, Michigan
www.cherrylakepublishing.com

Reading Adviser: Marla Conn MS, Ed., Literacy specialist, Read-Ability, Inc.
Book Designer: Felicia Macheske

Photo Credits: © Incredible Arctic/Shutterstock.com, cover; © Dr. John Cloud, NOAA Central Library, Historian/ Flickr CC BY 2.0, 5; © Bain News Service, Publisher. V. Stefansson. , . [No Date Recorded on Caption Card] Photograph. Retrieved from the Library of Congress, https://www.loc.gov/item/ggb2004007188/. (Accessed September 25, 2017.), 7; © Nathanxrx/Shutterstock.com, 8; © Mikhail Kolesnikov/Shutterstock.com, 11; © Tyler Olson/Shutterstock.com, 12; © Katvic/Shutterstock.com, 14; © Tyler Olson/Shutterstock.com, 17; © Africa Studio/Shutterstock.com, 19; © NEstudio/Shutterstock.com, 21; © Valsib/Shutterstock.com, 22; © VladKol/ Shutterstock.com, 25; © Loredo/iStock.com, 27; © Grafissimo/iStock.com, 28

Graphic Elements Throughout: © Gordan/Shutterstock.com; © adike/Shutterstock.com; © Yure/Shutterstock.com

45th Parallel Press is an imprint of Cherry Lake Publishing.

Library of Congress Cataloging-in-Publication Data has been filed and is available at catalog.loc.gov

Cherry Lake Publishing would like to acknowledge the work of The Partnership for 21st Century Skills.
Please visit *www.p21.org* for more information.

Printed in the United States of America
Corporate Graphics

table of contents

chapter one

Wrangel Island or Bust!

Who was Ada Blackjack? What was the expedition?

Ada Blackjack was born on May 10, 1898. She was born in Solomon, Alaska. She moved to Nome, Alaska. Nome was 30 miles (48 kilometers) away. At that time, Alaska wasn't part of the United States.

Blackjack got married. She had three children. She had a tough life. Two of her children died. Only her son lived. Her son was named Bennett. He was sick a lot. Her husband drowned. This left her very poor. She needed to make money. She needed to pay for Bennett's doctors. She put Bennett in an **orphanage**. Orphanages take care of children without parents. She was going to make money. She was going to come back for him.

In 2003, only four people lived in Solomon.

spotlight biography

Juana Maria is the "Lone Woman of San Nicolas Island." Her survival story inspired Scott O'Dell's book, *Island of the Blue Dolphins*. Russian hunters invaded her island. They killed most of her tribe. This happened in 1835. A church group took the survivors to the San Gabriel Mission. But Juana Maria was left behind. She lived on the island for 18 years. She survived by herself. She lived in a hut made of whalebones. She ate seals. She wore a dress made of bird feathers. George Nidever found her in 1853. He took her to the Santa Barbara Mission. Juana Maria lived there for 7 weeks. She got sick. She died.

Vilhjalmur Stefansson wanted to go across the Chukchi Sea. He wanted to go to Russia's Wrangel Island. Stefansson wanted to claim the island for Canada. He paid for an **expedition**. Expeditions are trips with goals.

Stefansson hired a team. The team had five people. Allan Crawford was from Canada. He was the leader. Fred Maurer was from the United States. So was Lorne Knight. Knight had explored the area before. Milton Galle was also from the United States. He had already been to Wrangel Island. His ship crashed there in 1914. Blackjack was also hired. She was to be a cook and **seamstress**. Seamstresses sew clothes.

Stefansson was a famous Arctic explorer.

Stefansson wanted to hire Alaskan families. He wanted women to make boots and clothes. He wanted men to hunt. But Blackjack was the only one who showed up for the job.

Blackjack was scared. She was 23 years old. She was barely 5 feet (152.4 centimeters) tall. She was shy. She didn't know what life was like beyond Nome. She was scared of guns. She was scared of polar bears. She didn't know how to live off the land. She didn't know how to build an **igloo**. Igloos are houses made of ice blocks. Blackjack wanted to quit.

◄ Wrangel Island is 85 miles (137 km) from Siberia.

chapter two

Hard Times

Why did Blackjack go on the expedition? What was Wrangel Island like?

The men didn't think Blackjack would survive. They doubted her. They made fun of her. But they needed her. They convinced her to go. They promised they'd stop at another city and hire others to take her place. They paid her $50 a month. She needed the money. So, she went.

It was hard to get a ship. No one wanted to go to the island. No one wanted to freeze. The team finally found a ship. Their ship was named *Silver Wave*.

Wrangel Island seemed far away and full of dangers, like polar bears.

They set sail on September 9, 1921. They planned to be away for 2 years. But they only brought enough food for 6 months. They planned on hunting for food. They planned on farming.

They arrived at Wrangel Island on September 16. Blackjack said, "The land looked very large to me. But they said that it was only a small island. I thought at first that I would turn back. But I decided it wouldn't be fair to the boys. Soon after we arrived, I started to sew."

The team built igloos.

explained by science

Alaska has many islands. It has chains of small islands. Volcanoes formed most of these islands. Volcanoes are tall like mountains. They open downward to pools of lava. Lava is melted rock and gases. Pressure builds up. Volcanoes erupt, or burst. They shoot out lava. Lava spills over the opening. These eruptions cause floods, earthquakes, and other disasters. They also form islands. Volcanic islands are created by Earth's plates moving over a lava flow. As the lava cools it builds on itself. The rock breaks the surface of the ocean. Islands are formed. Volcanoes are just one way islands are made.

Spring came. The men killed more than 30 seals. They killed 10 polar bears. They killed geese and ducks. They thought there'd be plenty of meat.

Summer came. Knight swam in a river. He went by himself. He got sick.

Fall came. Things got bad. They waited for a **supply** boat. Supply means things they need. This includes food. No boat came. There was too much ice.

On January 8, Knight and Crawford left for Siberia. They went to get help. But they returned in 3 weeks. Knight was too sick. He couldn't travel.

◄ Boats couldn't get through the ice to get to the island.

chapter three

All Alone

Why was Blackjack left alone? What happened to the team?

Winter came. There wasn't much to hunt. There wasn't enough **game** on the island. Game is any animal that can be hunted and eaten. They ran out of food. They were starving. They **rationed** the remaining food. Ration means to eat a little at a time.

On January 28, 1923, they needed a plan. Three men left to get help and food. They planned to walk 700 miles (1,126 km) across the frozen sea. They left Blackjack behind. Her job was to take care of Knight.

The men vowed to come back. They vowed to bring back a ship or a dog team. Blackjack never saw them again.

Expedition members must take care of each other in rough situations.

would you?

- **Would you live in Alaska?** Alaska is beautiful. It has mountains. It has lots of wildlife. There's much to do for people who like outdoor adventures. But winters are dark and cold. There aren't many people there. Alaskans are just 2 percent of the U.S. population. More caribou than people live in Alaska. More people live in Columbus, Ohio, than in all of Alaska.

- **Would you eat seals?** Eating seals is banned in many countries. Some people don't like how seals are hunted. Some countries allow the hunting of seals. Seal meat is lean. It has no fat. It tastes yummy to many people.

By February, Knight couldn't move. Blackjack made a bag of sand. She kept it at his feet. She did this to keep him warm. She sewed pillows from empty grain sacks. She stuffed them with cotton. This helped the sores on his body.

Knight was unkind. He said mean things to her. But she still nursed him. She didn't want to be alone. Any person was better than none.

Knight died that spring. Blackjack was on her own. She was scared. She was lonely.

Blackjack did have a cat with her. The cat's name was Vic.

chapter four

Learning to Live

How did Blackjack survive? How was she rescued?

Blackjack survived for months. She survived by herself. She survived in below-freezing weather. She learned new skills. She learned to use guns. She practiced. She hunted seals. She trapped foxes. She studied the animals' moves. She was smart.

Blackjack tried to leave the island. She made a boat out of seal skins. She used it twice. A wind caught it. The boat was lost. She made another boat. She used wood to make a frame. She cut up part of her tent. She sewed it onto the frame. This boat didn't work. She kept trying.

Blackjack used guns to hunt. She needed to eat.

Wrangel Island was the last place on Earth to have woolly mammoths.

Blackjack was rescued on August 19, 1923. This was 2 years after she arrived. A ship finally came to the island. The ship was called *Donaldson*.

Stefansson had hired Harold Noice. Noice's job was to pick up five people. Noice got to the island. He was surprised. He only found Blackjack alive.

Noice and Blackjack buried Knight. Then they returned to Nome. They guessed that the other men had died on the ice. They were never found.

survival tips

STRANDED ON AN ISLAND!

- Look for wreckage. Gather whatever you can. Find useful things.

- Find water that's safe to drink. Streams or rivers have fresh water. Drink raindrops on leaves. Don't drink salt water. Salt water is in oceans and seas.

- Look for plants. Water should be nearby.

- Dig down into the ground to find water.

- Make a shelter. Use logs. Use leaves.

- Make a rescue signal. Make smoke. Spell "help" with rocks.

- Look for fish close to the island. Make a spear by sharpening a stick. Spear the fish.

- Eat seaweed growing near the island. Don't eat seaweed that drifted to the island.

- Wait for help. Stay put. Moving around makes you hard to find.

chapter five

The Heroine of Wrangel Island

What happened to Blackjack when she returned? What did people think about her?

Blackjack returned home. She took Bennett to Seattle, Washington. She took him to see a doctor. She returned to Alaska. She got married again. She had another son. She named him Billy. She got divorced.

She was still poor. Billy and Bennett were placed in a home for 9 years. She made money. She took her sons back to Nome. She worked as a reindeer herder. She hunted and trapped for food.

She cared for Bennett her whole life. He was not healthy. She died at age 85. She died on May 29, 1983. She is buried in Anchorage, Alaska.

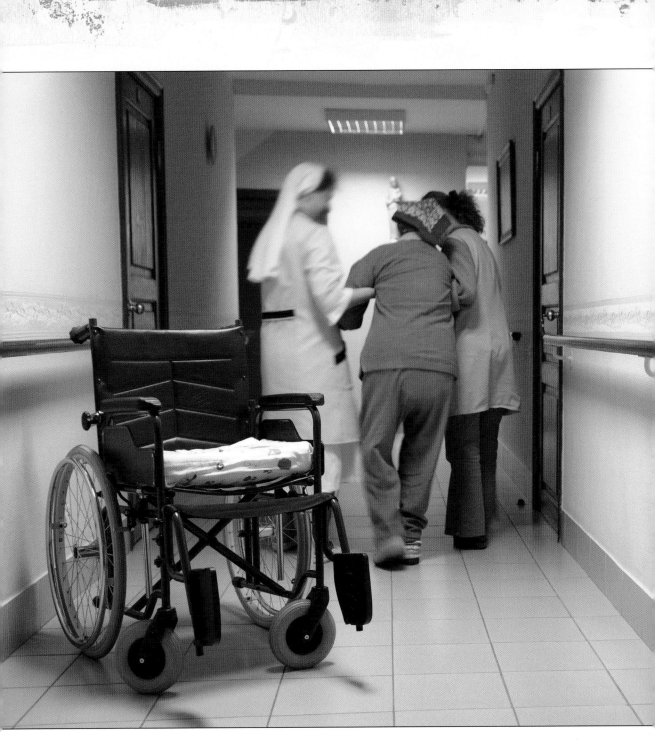

Blackjack died at the Pioneer Home.
This was a state home for older people.

Rest in Peace

Amelia Earhart was born in 1897. She was a famous aviator. Aviators fly planes. Earhart flew across the Atlantic Ocean. She did this by herself. She was the first woman to do this. In 1937, she tried to fly around the world. She disappeared over the Pacific Ocean. Nobody knows what happened to her. Some people believe she died in a plane crash. Some believe she survived an emergency landing. They believe she lived on a deserted island. They believe she lived for several weeks. They believe she died on the island. A human skeleton was found on the island. Scientists studied it. They think it's a match for Earhart. Her death is a mystery.

People were interested in her survival story. Blackjack got a lot of attention. She didn't like the attention. But Stefansson and Noice did. They made money off her story. Blackjack didn't get any money for her story. She got money for the expedition. She got some money for her furs. She used that money to help Bennett.

Some people blamed her for Knight's death. Blackjack didn't like that. This made her sad. Knight's parents met her. They supported Blackjack. They said she did all she could. But people still talked.

There were many newspaper stories about Blackjack.

Many people thought she was a hero. A newspaper said, "She had guts like a hero." She survived. More experienced men did not. Some newspapers called her a "female Robinson Crusoe." Robinson Crusoe is a famous book character. He also survived on an island.

Billy had a sign put on Blackjack's grave. The sign read, "The heroine of Wrangel Island."

Blackjack was more than a hero. She was a survivor!

◄ *Robinson Crusoe* was written by Daniel Defoe.

Did You Know?

- People have lived in Alaska for at least 15,000 years. These early people spread out over Alaska. They formed three main groups. The groups are Eskimos, Indians, and Aleuts.

- In the United States, seal blubber is fed to chickens.

- Blackjack's son Bennett had tuberculosis and spinal meningitis. These are serious illnesses.

- Stefansson said, "I think that anyone with good eyesight and a rifle can live anywhere in the Polar regions indefinitely." He compared the North Pole to Hawaii.

- Wrangel Island covers about 2,000 square miles (5,180 sq. km). It's 80 miles (129 km) long. It's 18 to 30 miles (29 to 48 km) wide. It's now a Russian wildlife park. It's surrounded by ice fields. It's covered in a thick fog.

- Blackjack tried to avoid polar bears. She was hunting seals. She barely escaped from a mother bear and her cub.

- Polar bears are only found in the Arctic. They're the largest land predators on Earth. Predators are hunters.

- Blackjack read Knight's Bible. It gave her hope.

- Blackjack's son Billy described her as a loving mother and a heroine in the history of Arctic exploration. He said, "She survived against all odds."

Consider This!

Take a Position: Read more about Wrangel Island. Do you think it was a good idea for Stefansson to want to claim it? Argue your point with reasons and evidence.

Say What? Blackjack had to learn survival skills. Challenge yourself to learn a new skill. Explain what this skill is. Explain how this skill will help you.

Think About It! Would you be able to survive on Wrangel Island? What skills do you have? What skills do you need? Are you more prepared than Blackjack was?

Learn More

- Caravantes, Peggy. *Marooned in the Arctic: The True Story of Ada Blackjack, the "Female Robinson Crusoe."* Chicago: Chicago Review Press, 2016.

- Niven, Jennifer. *Ada Blackjack: A True Story of Survival in the Arctic.* New York: Hyperion, 2003.

- Powell, Martin, and Eva Cabrera. *Daniel Defoe's Robinson Crusoe: A Graphic Novel.* North Mankato, MN: Stone Arch Books, 2016.

Glossary

expedition (ek-spuh-DISH-uhn) a trip with a purpose or goal

game (GAME) animals that can be hunted or eaten

igloo (IG-loo) a house built of ice blocks

orphanage (OR-fuh-nij) a home for children without parents

rationed (RASH-uhnd) allowed a certain amount

seamstress (SEEM-stris) a person who sews clothes

supply (suh-PLYE) resources and materials

Index

About the Author

Dr. Virginia Loh-Hagan is an author, university professor, former classroom teacher, and curriculum designer. She wants to visit Alaska one day. She lives in San Diego with her very tall husband and very naughty dogs. To learn more about her, visit www.virginialoh.com.